Valde Books

www.valdebooks.com - 2009

Parables of the Christ-life

by

I. Lilias Trotter

To

F.N.F. B.G.L.N. G.S.T. & A.M.E.

'fellow workers unto the kingdom of God.'

TABLE OF CONTENTS

Parables of the Christ-life

LIFE--the first glance would hardly find it on this African hillside in the summertime. The hot wind of the desert has passed over it, and the spring beauty of iris and orchid, asphodel and marigold, has vanished. Nothing is to be seen but the mellow golden-brown of the grass, broken by blue-green aloe leaves, and here and there a deep madder head of dried-up fennel.

Yet life is reigning, not death, all the while; it is there, in infinitely greater abundance than when the field was green--life enough to clothe a score of fields next year.

Stoop down and look into that withered grass, and a whole new world of God's handiwork will come into view in the burnt-up tangle. For of all the growing things out here, the seed-vessels are among the most wonderful. Even little insignificant plants that would hardly catch your eye when in flower, develop forms of quaint beauty as the capsules ripen. And now that all is finished, they lie stored with vitality in the midst of the seeming loss around.

Do you see the parable? We will trace it out step by step.

Back we must go, to the days of early spring. The annuals that clothed the field had each but one life then; a perishing life, though it looked so strong in its young vigour. Left to itself, it stood "condemned already."

But the critical moment came, changing its whole destiny, when a new birth took place: the vitalizing pollen was received by the pistil, and set up the reign of a fresh undying creation. All that had gone before in the plant's history was a preparation for this moment: all that followed was a working out to its fruition.

"Verily, verily I say unto thee, except a man be born again, he cannot see the Kingdom of God." Every soul carries like the flower a possible life, other than that of its first birth; more than that, to every soul within reach of the Gospel there comes probably a moment when the Life of God draws near and could be received if it were willing. There is a crisis like that which the flower reaches, when all things are ready. If that crisis is not seized, nothing lies before the plant but useless, irrevocable decay; the power to receive withers and vanishes; and nothing can renew it.

"That which is born of the flesh is flesh, and that which is born of the Spirit is spirit. Marvel not that I said unto thee, ye must be born again." "Flesh and blood cannot inherit the Kingdom of God, neither doth corruption inherit incorruption." Are you letting pass the moment on which all eternity hangs?

* * * * * *

The hour at which this new birth can take place in the flower is the hour at which the stigma is able to grasp the pollen that comes to it, blown by the wind or carried by the bees and butterflies. Up till then the grains fall off unheeded; but now it develops a surface, glutinous in some cases, velvety in others, that can clasp and keep them fast. The pollen grains lay hold at the same moment by their sculptured points and ridges. They "apprehend" each other, and the pollen, with its mysterious quickening power, does the rest. As soon as it is received it sinks down into the innermost depths of the flower's heart, and starts there the beginning of the new creation.

The most wonderful secrets of the plant world hang round the process of fertilisation, and the ways in which these springs of the second birth are guarded and set going, but the flower's simple work is to open and receive.

"The gift of God is eternal life"--oh, marvellous words!--"through Jesus Christ our Lord." "As many as received Him, to them gave He power to become the sons of God, even to them that believe on His name." "He that hath the Son hath life, and he that hath not the Son of God hath not life." "Behold I stand at the door and knock: if any man hear My voice and open the door, I will come in to him."

It is utterly, unbelievably simple. Receive Jesus with a heart-grasp, and you will find, like the flower, a spring of eternal life, entirely distinct from your own, that is perishing, set working deep down in your inmost being.

And all that is needed, for the fulfilment of God's uttermost purpose for you, is that this "new man" should be formed and that the old should pass away.

From the very outset of its new birth we see this double process going on in the plant. Within a few hours the throb of new life has spread through the flower, with this first result, that the petals begin to wither. Fertilisation marks the striking of the death-blow to all that went before. Look at a clover head; do you know why some of the spikes are upright and others turned downwards and fading? It is because these last have received the new tide, and the old is ebbing out already. The birth-peal and the death-knell rang together. Fertilisation marks the death of the flower and the death of the flower the death of the annual, though the carrying out of its doom comes gradually.

And in like manner the sentence of death passes, in the Cross, on the old nature in its entirety, as the new comes into being. This is the one only basis and groundwork for all carrying out in our practical experience of what that death means. Once for all let this be clear. Apart from the work done on Calvary, all working out of a death process in our own souls is only a false and dangerous mysticism... . "I have been

2

crucified with Christ." (R. V.)--Yes, long before ever I asked to be--glory be to God! and yet as freshly as if it were yesterday, for time is nowhere with Him.

And simultaneously, in figure, in the little flower-heart, while "that which is natural" begins to fade, "that which is spiritual" dawns. The seed-vessel with its hidden treasure--the ultimate object of this miracle of quickening--begins immediately to form. It was within three days of "the heavenly vision" when the once rejected Jesus was received by St. Paul, that the commission came--"he is a chosen vessel unto Me, to bear My Name." A chosen vessel unto Him. The seed-vessel belongs to the seed, only and for ever: it is formed for itself and has no purpose apart. Separation has nothing austere and narrow in it when it is unto Him.

Chosen vessels to bear His Name--His personality; with all that is wrapped up in that Name of fragrance and healing, authority and power; chosen to go about this weary sinful world with the living Christ folded in our hearts, ready and able as of old to meet the need around. Is not this a calling for which it is worth counting, as St. Paul did, all things but loss?

Chosen vessels--there is the vessel and there is the treasure in it, for ever distinct, though in wonderful union, like the seed-vessel and the seed: the one enshrines the other.

God builds up a shrine within us of His workmanship, from the day in which Jesus was received. The seed-vessel is its picture. With the old nature He can have nothing to do except to deliver it to death: no improving can fit it for His purpose, any more than the leaf or tendril, however beautiful, can be the receptacle of the seed. There must be "a new creation" (R.V., margin), "the new man," to be the temple of the Divine Life.

And as the petals drop off, and the growing seed-vessel comes into view, we see a fresh individuality developed. Compare in these four pages some of the seed-vessels of a single family--vetch and clover: we found over thirty species of it in that one field of the frontispiece. These will show something of their extraordinary variety-- we have bunches of horns great and small, and bunches of imitation centipedes, and bunches of mock holly leaves, prickly coils and velvety balls; mimic concertinas, and bits of quaint embroidery; imitation snail-shells, croziers, pods with frills at the seams, spiked caskets with curious indentations, clusters of stars, bladders like soft paper, and plaited spirals wound into a tiny cocoanut, that, untwisted, becomes a minature crown of thorns--are they not all a visible expression of the thoughts that are more than can be numbered? And the greater part spring from little unnoticeable flowers, so alike in their yellow or pink that you have to look closely in order to find out any difference! It is the seed-bearing that gives them their individual character.

And the same God has manifold plans for our development too, as vessels for His Christ-life. It is by the Divine indwelling that our true, eternal personality dawns, and for the expression of the special manifestation of Himself which is entrusted to each one of us. The protoplasm that quickens each different seed is one and the same essence, but in no two does it find the same expression. He needs the whole Church to manifest His whole character and accomplish His appointed ministry, and so the individual development must differ widely in everything but the common vital principle. Life--eternal life--is the essence of all--life receiving and life-giving. There is no need to imitate the seed-vessel of a brother vetch!--only to draw into our own the fulness of grace that we may develop into its full individuality the mission entrusted to us.

There is nothing arbitrary in these differing shapes of the seed-vessels. If we look closely, we shall find that they are formed in union with the seed that each contains-- it is this that determines the form of each, and builds it up. See these few instances: the peas need their long pod with its daintily-cushioned divisions, to allow each little globe to round itself to perfection; the crescent-shaped seeds of this other vetch, each set into its own place again, form the distinctive character of their different sheath--so do the tiny rod-shaped ones of the third vetch, which clothe themselves in a segmented rod in turn. While on the other hand the fine sand-like grain of this snap-dragon needs storing in a capsule--such a quaint one it is (whether most like a bird or a mouse sitting on a twig is hard to say)--but it is a perfectly adapted treasure-bag for the delicate things, and when they are ripe the two eyes open, and the wind shakes the seed out by them! Each one lays itself out for the special trust committed to it. Is it not the same wonderful Fashioner Who fits us and our ministry together, and forms us through it with unerring precision, preparing us for the white stone and the new name which no man knoweth saving he that receiveth it, eternity's seal on the heavenly individuality of each. That eternal future will show how the Lord had need of each of us in our varying character, and how all that made up this earthly life fitted us for "bearing about" the special manifestation of Jesus entrusted to us, in which no other could take our place. He needs us, every one of us, as if there were no other besides.

* * * * * *

But we will go back from this glimpse of God's ultimate purpose for us, to watch the process by which it is reached, so far as we can trace it in the ripening of the little annuals.

The figure will not give us all the steps by which God gets His way in the intricacies of a human soul: we shall see no hint in it of the cleansing and filling that is needed in sinful man before he can follow the path of the plant. It shows us some of the Divine principles of the new life rather than a set sequence of experience; above all, the parable gives a lesson that most of us only begin to learn after Pentecost has become a reality to us--the lesson of walking, not after the flesh, but after the Spirit.

The flesh--the life of nature--is all, good and bad alike, that we had and were before Christ came to us. We see its shadow in the life of root and stem, leaf and tendril and petal, that made up the plant before its new birth took place; "for all flesh is grass, and all the goodliness thereof is as the flower of the field." It is not only that which is sinful as opposed to that which is holy: it is that which is human as opposed to that which is Divine.

In the earlier stage of the seed-vessel's growth we see the two lives, the old and the new, practically going on alongside. And can we not remember, many of us, in our own history, how the self life went almost untouched and unrecognised, for years, while all the time Christ was growing within us, and our ministry was being given?

Let us look at the seed-vessels, well set and forming fast, with their natural life all unbroken as yet, and learn to be very tender and patient with the early stages of God's work in those around.

But though the two may exist for a time side by side, they cannot flourish together. The crisis must come to us as to the annual, when the old creation begins to go down into the grave, and the new begins to triumph at its cost.

In the plant life the two are absolutely and for ever separate--there is no possibility of confounding the perishable existence of leaf and stalk with the newborn seed-vessel and its hidden riches. In the heavenly light the distinction stands out as ineffaceably. "That which is born of the flesh is flesh, and that which is born of the Spirit is spirit." But our eyes are too dim at first to distinguish them in detail: with most of us it is only when the cleansing Blood has dealt with the question of known sin, and the Spirit's incoming has cleared our vision, that the two lives, natural and spiritual, begin to stand out before us, no longer shading into each other, but in vivid contrast. The word of God in the hand of the Holy Ghost pierces to the dividing asunder of soul and spirit, and we see bit by bit as we can bear it, how we have made provision for the flesh, given occasion to the flesh, had confidence in the flesh, warred after the flesh, judged after the flesh, purposed after the flesh, known each other after the flesh. The carnal nature with its workings stands out as the hindrance in the way of the Divine, and the time comes when we see that no more growth is possible to the Christ in us unless a deliverance comes here.

We are helpless in the matter. There is no system of self-repression or self-mortification that will do anything but drive the evil below the surface, there to do a still more subtle work, winding down out of reach. The roots will only strike deeper and the sap flow stronger for the few leaves trimmed off here and there. If self sets to

5

work to slay self it will only end in rising hydra-headed from the contest. How is the deliverance to come?

The annuals give us the secret. Look back at the vetch seed-vessels. Why is it that the leaves which used to stand firm and fresh like those of the flowering clover, have begun to shrivel and turn yellow? It is because they have acquiesced wholly now in the death sentence of their new birth, and they are letting the new life live at the expense of the old. Death is being wrought out by life.

And the same triumphant power of the new life is set free as we come to accept to its utmost limits the sentence of Calvary, that "our old man was crucified with Him," in its sum-total, seen and unseen, root and branch. Christ is our Life now--our only Life--and we begin to find that He is dealing with the old creation, we hardly know how. We only know that as we bring the judgment, the motive, the aim that were ours, not His, into contact with Him, they shrivel and wither like the dying leaves. The impulses and the shrinkings of the flesh perish in His Presence alike. The new life wrecks the old. "If ye through the Spirit do mortify the deeds of the body ye shall live"--that is what the withering leaves say. We are "saved by His life."

The great North African aloe plant shows this very strikingly. It is like our annuals on a large scale, for it flowers and seeds but once in its career, though that numbers more years than these can count weeks.

Up till then its thick hard leaves look as if nothing could exhaust their vigour. The flower stalk pushes up from a fresh sheaf of them--up and up twelve or fourteen feet--and expands into a candelabra of golden blossom, and not a droop comes in the plant below. But as the seed forms, we see that life is working death, slowly and surely; the swords lose their stiffness and colour and begin to hang helplessly, and by the time it is ripe, every vestige of vitality is drained away from them, and they have gone to limp, greyish-brown streamers. The seed has possessed itself of everything.

And the meadow plants that we have been watching follow, on their small pattern, the same law.

All gives way to the ripening seed. In the grasses the very root perishes by the time the grain is yellow, and comes up whole if you try to break the stem. They "reign in life" above through the indwelling seed, while all that is "corruptible" goes down into dust below. They have let all go to life--the enduring life: they are not taken up with the dying--that is only a passing incident--everything is wrapped up into the one aim, that the seed may triumph at any cost. Death is wrought out almost unconsciously: the seed has done it all.

Can we not trace the same dealing in our souls as, slowly, tenderly, all that nourished that which is carnal is withdrawn, giving way to the forming of the Christ life in its place? His thoughts and desires and ways begin to dethrone ours as the aloe seed dethrones its leaves and casts them to the ground. "He must increase, but I must decrease."

And the outward dealings co-operate with the inward. It is just in the very corner of everyday life where God has put us, that this can take place, and the surrounding influences can have their share in bringing down to death the old nature. It is no mystical, imaginary world that draws out the latent forms of self, but the commonplace, matter-of-fact world about us.

It is in contact with others, for the most part, that the humbling discoveries of the workings of the flesh come, on the one hand, and on the other we find ourselves breaking down in one after another of our strongest points. And all these things that seem against us are really doing a blessed work--they are "the Wind of the Lord" coming "up from the wilderness" to "spoil the treasure" of all that is of former days. Everything that is "natural," good and bad alike, must go down into death before its blast, when God takes it in hand--all that we can lean upon in outward things, all clinging to the visible and the transitory; and with this result, that our arms clasp closer and closer round the Eternal Seed, Christ in us the Hope of Glory--known no longer after the flesh, but by the mighty revelation of the Holy Ghost.

All this is shadowed forth in the story of these southern plants; one day's sirocco in May will turn a field, bright with the last flowers, into a brown wilderness, where the passing look sees nothing but ruin--yet in that one day the precious seed will have taken a stride in its ripening that it would have needed a month of ordinary weather to bring about; it will have drawn infinite life out of the fiery breath that made havoc with the outward and visible.

"The grass withereth, the flower fadeth, because the Spirit of the Lord bloweth upon it." But "our light affliction" (and from the context we see that spiritual trial is included there) "which is but for a moment, worketh for us a far more exceeding and eternal weight of glory--while we look not at the things which are seen, but at the things which are not seen; for the things which are seen are temporal, but the things which are not seen are eternal." In all the breaking down on the human side, the hidden treasure is left not only unhurt but enriched. Everything that wrecks our hopes of ourselves, and our earthly props, is helping forward infinitely God's work in us.

So "we faint not; but though our outward man perish, yet the inward man is renewed day by day." God's purpose for us is that we should be seed-vessels; all the rest may go down into nothingness, for it "profiteth nothing." The plant does not faint in its inner heart. Little does it matter what happens to the "corruptible": each fading of the outward only marks a corresponding development of the "incorruptible" within.

"What things were gain to me" (the words seem echoed from the fading leaves and the ripening seed), "those I counted loss for Christ. Yea, doubtless, and I count all things but loss, for the excellency of the knowledge of Christ Jesus my Lord: for whom I have suffered the loss of all things, and do count them but dung, that I may win Christ."

"This one thing I do." "They that are after the flesh do mind the things of the flesh; but they that are after the Spirit, the things of the Spirit." The plant has nothing to "mind" now but the treasure it bears. Its aim has grown absolutely simple. In old days there was the complexity of trying to carry on two lives at once, nourishing root and stem, leaf and flower and tendril, alongside the seed-vessel and the seed. All that is over. It withdraws itself quietly into the inner shrine where God is working out that which is eternal. It has chosen, in figure, that good part which shall not be taken away: it is pressing towards the mark for the prize of its calling.

Pressing, but in perfect rest. "They toil not, neither do they spin," these plants, in their seed-bearing any more than in their flowering. And when we have learnt something of their surrender, we are ready for their secret of waiting on God's inworking. How long we are in grasping that we are His workmanship, even as they--in discovering the simple fact that it is exactly as impossible by our own striving to develop the Christ-life in our hearts as to form the seed in the pod! We have not to produce out of our higher nature a lowliness and a patience and a purity of our own, but simply to let the pure, patient, lowly life of Jesus have its way in us by yieldingness to it and by faith in its indwelling might. "All that God wants from man is opportunity." The whole of our relationship to His power, whether for sanctification or for service, is summed up in those words.

Surrender--stillness--a ready welcoming of all stripping, all loss, all that brings us low, low into the Lord's path of humility--a cherishing of every whisper of the Spirit's voice, every touch of the prompting that comes to quicken the hidden life within: that is the way God's human seed-vessels ripen, and Christ becomes "magnified" even through the things that seem against us.

"Mine but to be still: Thine the glorious power, Thine the mighty will."

And it is not only the siroccos that help forward His purpose for us! The "clear heat" and the midnight dews all minister together: "the sun to rule the day" when His light and sweetness flood our souls;--the darkness--the cloudless darkness--of a walk by faith when "the moon and the stars" of the promises alone are visible: "His mercy endureth for ever" through all alike and He uses them to their utmost that Christ may be formed in us.

For the spirit of abandonment has to be carried into our spiritual life, as well as into the things that only touch the natural. The seed-vessel has to go down into death as well as the leaf. Look at it as it begins to pass into the valley of that shadow and its strength begins to ebb away. It is only getting ready by its weakening, for the service to which it has been called.

Long ago we imagined, it may be, an enduement of power from on high in which we should have a conscious supply of the heavenly energising--a conscious equipment for every service--a reservoir of Divine might that could be drawn on at will. But watch the seed-vessel as the hour comes near in which its ministry can be fulfilled; there is only weakness greater than ever before. "It is sown in weakness"; only in the raising does the power come into play.

"I was with you in weakness and in fear and in much trembling. And my speech and my preaching was not with enticing words of man's wisdom, but in demonstration of the Spirit and of power: that your faith should not stand in the wisdom of men, but in the power of God." "The weak things of the world hath God chosen." "We are weak with Him" (margin)--oh! words of wonderful grace and sweetness. There is nothing but rest in being brought low "with Him."

And not only must our service feel this weakening touch: it must go deeper yet. Our experiences, the blessed hours of opened heavens, must be held with a loose hand. We saw the life withdrawn before from the leaves of the old creation into the seed-vessel of the new. Now it is withdrawn further still, as ripeness comes, from the seed-vessel into the seed. In the early stages of Christian path we are apt to be much taken up, and rightly, with the spiritual processes by which God is working in us. But in the "ripeness of maturity" (the real sense of "perfect" in Col. i. 28, and elsewhere) He has something better for us. "I live; yet not I, but Christ liveth in me." He wants to bring us from clinging to the emotional on one hand, and on the other from morbid introspection: for perhaps one of the chief dangers besetting those who are following hard after Him, lies in getting taken up with these inner experiences (it is awfully possible for the devil to rivet the chains of self back on a soul even in the very act of watching the death process going on within it, getting it absorbed even with its own dying!). Let us come as fast as we can to letting the seed-vessel go as well as the leaves, God wants to bring us to a life of childlike simplicity, taken up with His Christ; always lower and lower at His feet in the consciousness of shortcoming and unworthiness as His Glory shines, but with our spiritual selves and all their intricacies fading out of sight before Him. As we go on, we learn to draw the supply of every need for spirit and soul and body from the simplest, barest, most direct contact with Him. All the intervening tissues in the seed-vessel melt away. "You have learnt the death of self when there is nothing between your bare heart and Jesus."

Yes; when the seed is ripe it fills up the whole of the husk--there is no room left for anything else: the walls shrivel to a mere shell. This is the calling of the Bride--to have no room for anything but Jesus. Blessed are they who hear it and respond.

Look at the parable. The life of leaf and tendril has shrunk away, but there is nothing sad about the dying of the seed-vessel. What lovely things they are, these little burnt offerings! Their bright golden browns look far happier than the greens of spring.

And they have come now to a point of beautiful heedless freedom about the future. When once the last shade of green that marks a clinging to the old days has vanished, all carefulness for the earthly side of things vanishes too. No matter how soon now the last strand of earthly support and supply gives way: its loss is not felt. The life is "hid" with such a hiding that nothing from around can touch it. The fiercest summer glow only causes the little germ to wrap itself close together in happy recklessness, the careless feet that tread it down can only hasten the burial that is its next stage onward, the autumn storms can bring it nothing but fresh draughts of quickening.

Yes, our life is hid with Christ in God, in actual truth as well in God's purpose, if it has come to this that it is "no longer" we that live but Christ that liveth in us. Oh! the simplicity of that "no longer"--as the seed-vessel pictures it now, taken up with the seed it bears, and heedless of itself and whatever may come. And yet, in the absolute simplicity, there is a depth of mystery that the former days never knew. It is like a soul that has come into the Holiest, where it has God alone.

* * * * * *

And now we turn to the other side, to watch what God can do, in the world around, with the Christ-life that He creates in us. We have seen its in-flowing: we will follow its outflow. To be to Jesus all for which He has called us--letting Him have His way utterly with us, possessed by Him, taken up with Him--that is the first purpose for our souls. But the Father's plan for us reaches wider than that, though it can reach no deeper. "The first Adam was made a living soul; the last Adam was made a quickening Spirit." His ultimate aim is to set free for His own use that which He has wrought in us in secret, and to give us the power of communicating that Divine life of which we have been made partakers. We are to be "good stewards of the manifold grace of God," entrusted with "the true riches" to minister for Him--His for His spending. The promise to Abraham: "I will bless thee ... and thou shalt be a blessing," gives the double purpose for His people--"grace" for our own souls, and "apostleship" for those around.

We have seen in parable, in the seed's growing and ripening, the work of the Spirit within us, forming the life of Jesus, and bringing down the flesh into the grave. In its scattering we see shadowed forth the Spirit upon us in His power of reaching other souls. There is no needs be with us that this double work should be consecutive as in the plants--it may go on simultaneously. There is never a moment, from the first receiving of Christ as Saviour, when the full outpouring of the Holy Ghost may not take place--never a moment when, in figure, the seed may not be set free. There are some few who leap down, as soon as they are saved, to the simple, bare, lowly faith which liberates God's power, and He can use them mightily all along, but they are very few. Practically in most cases there is time involved, because we take so long to unlearn our own sufficiency and our own resources, and even after we have received the promise of the Spirit through faith, we are puzzled, it may be, by a want of continuity in His outflow.

It is because, before God can get us to the place where He can send Him through us in a steady tide, we have to go lower than we dreamed of at first: and He may have to stop using us for a time, that He may deepen this work within, and bring us to utter brokenness.

Look at the last stage in the plant, before the inwrought life is free for use. There is a breaking-up and a breaking-down such as it never had before. Such brittleness comes as the seed ripens that it is almost impossible to pick some of the stems without cracking them in two or three places. The ripened seed-vessels share the same brittleness: you can hardly touch them without the whole crown falling to pieces in your hand.

Conscious weakness, as a preparation for service, is one thing: brokenness is another. We may know that we are but earthen pitchers, like Gideon's, with nothing of our own but the light within, and yet we may not have passed through the shattering that sheds the light forth.

This does not mean something vague or imaginary, but intensely practical. Read the description that Paul gives of the life of ministry--the apostolic life--and see what it is to be a shattered seed-vessel; it is no dreamy experience in the clouds!

"Let a man so account of us, as of the ministers of Christ, and stewards of the mysteries of God.... . We are made a spectacle to the world, and to angels, and to men. We are fools for Christ's sake, but ye are wise in Christ; we are weak, but ye are strong; ye are honourable, but we are despised. Even unto this present hour we both hunger and thirst and are naked and have no certain dwelling-place. And labour, working with our own hands: being reviled, we bless; being persecuted, we suffer it, being defamed, we intreat; we are made as the filth of the world, and are the offscouring of all things unto this day."

"Seeing we have this ministry, as we have received mercy, we faint not.... . But we have this treasure in earthen vessels, that the excellency of the power may be of God, and not of us. We are troubled on every side, yet not distressed; we are perplexed, but not in despair; persecuted, but not forsaken; cast down, but not destroyed; always bearing about in the body the dying of the Lord Jesus, that the life also of Jesus might be made manifest in our body. For we which live are alway delivered unto death for Jesus' sake, that the life also of Jesus might be made manifest in our mortal flesh."

"In all things approving ourselves as the ministers of God, in much patience, in afflictions, in necessities, in distresses, in stripes, in imprisonments, in tumults, in labours, in watchings, in fastings. ... By honour and dishonour, by evil report and good report: as deceivers and yet true; as unknown and yet well known; as dying, and behold we live; as chastened and not killed; as sorrowful, yet alway rejoicing; as poor, yet making many rich; as having nothing, and yet possessing all things."

"Are they ministers of Christ? (I speak as a fool) I am more; in labours more abundant, in stripes above measure, in prisons more frequent, in deaths oft. Of the Jews five times received I forty stripes save one. Thrice was I beaten with rods, once was I stoned, thrice I suffered shipwreck, a night and a day I have been in the deep; in journeyings often, in perils of waters, in perils of robbers, in perils by mine own countrymen, in perils by the heathen, in perils in the city, in perils in the wilderness, in perils in the sea, in perils among false brethren; in weariness and painfulness, in watchings often, in hunger and thirst, in fastings often, in cold and nakedness. Besides those things that are without, that which cometh upon me daily, the care of all the churches... . I take pleasure in infirmities, in necessities, in persecutions, in distresses for Christ's sake: for when I am weak, then am I strong."

Do you notice that in each passage these are given as the marks of "ministry"? Such were what Paul found to be the conditions of spiritual power. Their absence among us may account for its absence too! Oh! how little we know of them in the midst of the spirit of luxury that is around us in the world and of the easy-going Christianity of the Church! We cannot all be honoured by our service finding the same outward expression as his, in its bodily stress and suffering, but is there among us even a seeking after its spirit?

"This is sacrifice, 'death in us, life in you.'--In us, emptiness, weakness, suffering, pressure, perplexity. In you life--life--life! As if Paul would say, 'the more I am pressed above measure, the more the life of Jesus is abundant in its outflow, and in its quickening of other lives.' This is the apostolic life. Through the Eternal Spirit, Christ offered Himself to God. Through the same Spirit shall we be enabled to walk in His steps, and to rejoice in ... sufferings ... and fill up ... that which is lacking of the afflictions of Christ in my flesh for His body's sake, which is the Church.'" [footnote*:"The Message of the Cross"--Mrs. Penn-Lewis.]

Yes, it is a broken spirit that we need--a spirit keeping no rights before God or man, longing to go down, down, anywhere, if other souls may be blessed. It is an indefinable thing, this brokenness, and yet it is as unmistakable when it has been wrought, as that of the seed-vessel in the field.

God has His promise for those "who sow in tears": those to whom to be a channel of Divine communication to the world means soul burden and travail. It is they who are bound to "reap in joy."

And as we look at these broken-up seed-vessels, we can read a warning as to our dealings with others, as well as the lesson to ourselves. If such brokenness as this is the condition of God's power upon us, what of the danger of making much of the instruments that He uses? If we do so even in thought, it will unconsciously show itself in manner and tone, and the subtle influence may reach them and be used of the devil to build again in a moment that which God had been long breaking down, and so stay the tide He had at last with infinite pains set free. "Who then is Paul, and who is Apollos, but ministers by whom ye believed, even as the Lord gave to every man? I have planted, Apollos watered; but God gave the increase. So then neither is he that planteth anything, neither he that watereth; but God that giveth the increase."

* * * * * *

And now we can turn at last to see in our picture-book the result of all this fading and stripping and breaking: no outcome as yet that will catch the eye of sense, yet full of eternal possibilities.

What a marvel it is, this seed "endynamited" for its ministry! Just an atom of whiteness, folded up in its smooth brown shell. Opposite p. 35 you see the two tiny specks in the splitting pod; does it not seem incredible that anything can come out of them? Could we imagine anything more insignificant? And yet they are brimful of a vitality that will last (given the necessary conditions) "while the earth remaineth," through harvest after harvest in ever-widening circles.

Equally unimportant from the point of view of "the natural man" is the heavenly seed that God gives His people to scatter. "The things of the Spirit of God ... are foolishness unto him." "The kingdom of God cometh not with observation." His beginnings are always very feeble things.

It is out of the hour of its greatest apparent extremity, moreover, that the seed launches out to its ministry. There was a time, a few weeks earlier, when you could, if you examined it, trace the future plant in embryo; the two seed-leaves and the rootlet were all visible in shades of exquisite green; but all this dries up when maturity comes, till there is not a sign of life left in it. Everything that is brilliant and beautiful is withdrawn and shrouded in the "bare grain" when we strip off the sheath and hold it in our hand: everything has gone down in defiant faith to the last ebb. Nothing is left to it, as far as we can discern, but the invisible, miracle-working power of God. Shall we not learn of the dried-up seed, to rejoice when in our seed-sowing we are shut up to God alone--when every shade of hope and promise to the eyes of sense, have faded like the baby seed-leaves in the germ? "So is the kingdom of God, as if a man should cast seed into the ground; and should sleep, and rise night and day, and the seed should spring and grow up, he knoweth not how."

To sow heavenly seed means to give way to Him in the promptings that are sure to come as soon as He finds us broken enough for Him to be able to send them. It is a direct passing on of that which comes to us from God, stripped of all self-effort: the message spoken "not in the words which man's wisdom teacheth, but which the Holy Ghost teacheth": the work done "striving according to His working which worketh in us mightily": the prayer that knows not what it should pray for as it ought, and yields itself to His "intercession for us with groanings that cannot be uttered." These are the things which, small as they are in this world's count, have the very pulse of eternity beating through them. Nothing but that which He inspires can carry quickening power: no experience--no spirituality even, can set the spark alight. It is not the seed-vessel that can do the work, any more than a bit of leaf-stalk or flower petal, but simply and only the seed. "It is the Spirit that quickeneth." "I believe in the Holy Ghost, the Lord and Giver of Life." Hallelujah!

Let us watch the seed-shedding, and see what it can teach us about sowing to the Spirit.

* * * * * *

There is a definite moment at which the seed is ripe for being liberated--that is the first thing we notice: and at that moment it is absolutely ready for its work. The storing of the nourishment for the young plant began on the very day when the new life entered the flower long ago, and it is finished now. All prepared too are the hooks, or spikes, or gummy secretions, needed to anchor it to the ground, and so to give a purchase to the embryo shoot when the time comes for it to heave its tombstone and come out to the light. Even its centre of gravity is so adjusted that, in falling from the sheath, the germ is in the very best position for its future growth. If it is torn out of the husk a day too soon, all this marvellous preparation will be wasted and come to nothing.

Can we not read our parable? How often we have had an impulse or a plan which we knew to be of God, with a flash of intuition, or with a gathering certainty: and the temptation has come to carry it straight off by ourselves, without waiting His time-- the very temptation that beset the Master in the wilderness.

Oh! let us learn of Him the lesson of letting God's seed-purposes ripen!--they can bear no fruit till they have come to their maturity: we shall but waste all He was preparing if we drag it out before its time. And only in a path in which we are learning to do nothing of ourselves but what we see the Father do, can we know when His hour is come. How accurately Jesus knew it! "I go not up yet unto this feast, for My time is not yet full come," He said to His brethren--and yet in a day

14

or two He was there. "Mine hour is not yet come," He said to His mother, when it was only a question of minutes. And by what marvellous insight He recognised the dawning of that final "hour" when He was asked for by those nameless Greeks--a hint of the ingathering of the travail of His soul! God can give us the same Divine instinct, when He has weaned us from our natural energy and impatience. And when His hour has struck, the whole powers of the world to come will be set free in the tiny helpless seed. "One day is with the Lord as a thousand years." He is a God worth waiting for!

And there is another thing closely linked with this patience in the seed-shedding. As we watch it going on in nature, we see how it is all done in cooperation with the forces at work outside itself. The wind knocks off and tosses away the dainty shutde-cocks of the scabious as they ripen one by one, and the pods wait for the hot touch of the sun to split them with the sudden contracting twist that sends the grains flying, like stones from a sling.

More wonderfully still we see this "working together" in the seeding of the cranesbill. The seeds stand together as they ripen, like arrows in a quiver, with their points downwards, and their feathered shafts straight up. When the time for action comes, the sun-heat peels them off, from below and above, so quickly that you can see them cue under your eyes, and turn into a spiral by their continued contractions. They fall, spike downward, by the weight of the seed, and the sun finishes the work he began. Closer still the gimlet winds, and as it does so it bores down into the hardest soil: and such is their strange power of penetration, as they are driven in, spite of all their weakness, that they bury themselves up to the very hilt, leaving only the last long curve flat on the surface. Then this snaps off, and leaves the head deep hidden. The spear-like grass you see opposite p. 40 follows the same rule: it is so sensitive to the heat that even the warmth of one's hand will set it twisting and thrusting its barb in. Cannot we trust the God Who planned them, to give us arrows that will be sharp in the hearts of His enemies, and to drive them home? At each fresh adaptation of the plants to their aim, we hear an echo of the words of Jesus, "Shall He not much more clothe you, O ye of little faith?"

And the restfulness of waiting God's hour for seed-shedding deepens as we learn to recognise the outward dealings of the Spirit as well as the inward, and watch the marked way in which He co-operates with the setting free of every seed as it ripens--how He brings across our path the soul who needs the very lesson He has just been teaching us--how the chance comes with perfect naturalness of reaching another over whom we have been longing. If our eyes are up, and our hands are off--if we learn to "wait on our ministering" like the seeds, in utter dependence on Him, we shall be able constantly to trace the Lord's working with us, and we shall have done with all the old restless striving to make opportunities--"We are labourers together with God."

Yes, it all centres round that question of quietness. "Opportunity" is given to every seed in its turn, as they lie in their layers in the capsule, or side by side in the pod. Not one forces its way forward, or gets in the way of another. Look at the exquisite fitting in any seed-vessel that you pull to pieces: the seeds are as close as they will go, but fenced off from crowding on each other and hindering each other's growth. He who packed them can be trusted, surely, with the arranging of our lives, that nothing may jostle in them, and nothing be wasted, for we are "of more value" to Him than these. If our days are a constant rush and hurry, week in and week out, there is grave reason to doubt if it is all God-given seed that we are scattering. He will give us no more to do than can be done with our spirits kept quiet and ready and free before Him.

Quiet and ready and free--that is another lesson that the seeds teach us. Off they go at a touch, at the moment when the inward preparedness and the outward opportunity coalesce. See the tiny corkscrews of the pink geranium in our meadow (a miniature of its blue brother the cranesbill). Look at the poise of them--and then at the sheaf of spears of this bit of grass, holding themselves freer still, and the downy head alongside, equally ready either to hold together or to fly with a breath ... and then look at our lives and see whether that is their attitude towards the Holy Ghost. Is there a soul poise that corresponds?

Oh! the pains that God has to take to bring us to this happy, childlike "abandon," equally ready for silence, or for saying or doing unhesitatingly the next thing He calls for, unfettered by surroundings or consequences. How much reserve and self-consciousness have to give way with some of us, before the absolute control passes into His Hands, and the responsibility with it! Then only can we know the "liberty," the "boldness," the "utterance" of Pentecost. "Whithersoever the Spirit was to go they went, thither was their spirit to go:" that is "the perfect law of liberty."

Yes, and that brings us a step further in the teachings of the seed-shedding. Off they go now, "every one straight forward"--off and onward to the place appointed. Look at the golden plough of the wild oat, with every spike and hair so set that it slips forwards and will not be pushed backwards. Look at the hooks and the barbs that cling to anything and everything that passes by if only they can carry their seed away and away. Look at the balls and the wheels that roll before the wind, and the parachutes and baby shuttlecocks that sail upon it: they all have a passion for getting far off, and they only show us a few of the numberless devices by which the same end is reached in plants of all lands.

Do you know why they want to scatter? It is because God planned the rotation of crops, long before it ever entered a farmer's brain! Around the parent stem the soil is exhausted of the chemical elements that were used in building it up, and if the seeds all fell straight down there, they could not reach their full development; so they have all these devices for travelling far away, where in supplying the needs of the barren places, their own are met It was even so with Jesus, God's "Corn of Wheat": did He not need this needy world to bring out His love and power? are not our empty hearts now "the riches of His inheritance"?

And the Christ-life in us, developed and set free, will go by its very nature reaching out and spending itself wherever there is want, in love and longing for the bare places and the far-off. The Spirit will carry our hearts and sympathies and prayers away and beyond the tiny circle around us, of our personal interests and our own work, into fellowship with the Father about the world He loves--fellowship with the Son over the Church for which He gave Himself: "not seeking our own profit, but the profit of many, that they may be saved." Perhaps He will carry us away our very selves, to some waste corner!

"He that soweth sparingly shall reap also sparingly; and he that soweth bountifully shall reap also bountifully. Let each man do according as he had purposed in his heart; not grudgingly, or of necessity, for God loveth a cheerful giver. And God is able to make all grace abound unto you; that ye, having always all sufficiency in everything, may abound unto every good work: as it is written, He hath scattered abroad, He hath given to the poor; His righteousness abideth for ever. And He that supplieth seed to the sower and bread for food, shall supply and multiply your seed for sowing, and increase the fruits of your righteousness: ye being enriched in everything unto all liberality, which worketh through us thanksgiving to God" (R.V.).

And as part of the enriching in everything unto all liberality, God can give us all the ingenuity of love in scattering broadcast Spirit-filled, Spirit-sent seed that He has figured in the seed-vessels--the heaven-given inspiration as to how to lay out His treasures to their uttermost--how to secure to Him the highest return out of our lives, as they do.

Yes, the "return" is to Him, as again we see in parable with the plants. They show us a love that seeketh not her own: no one knows whence the seeds come when they reach their journey's end: no glory can possibly gather round the plants that surrendered their lives to form and shed them. They just give and give, with no aim but to be bare footstalks when all is done. Everything is loosened and spent without a shade of calculation or self-interest.

"Not unto us, O Lord, not unto us, but unto Thy name give glory," they are all saying in spirit: they teach us absolute indifference as to whether our service is appreciated or even recognised, so long as the work is done and the Lord is glorified. The plant itself asks for nothing to keep, nothing to show, nothing to glory in from its whole life toil.

Nothing to glory in--God cannot get His whole glory while man gets any. That seems a truism, but do we realise the fact? "Herein is My Father glorified, that ye bear much fruit." If that is our one aim, as it was in the soul of Jesus, it is bound to be realised. Let Him work this in us too--this simple, absolute, absorbing passion of His years on earth.

And then we shall have, as He had, that independence of visible results that we have just seen in the plants. He left the world--this one world out of His mighty universe in which God had come to dwell--with no more to be seen from His travail than a few hundred brethren, every one of whom had forsaken Him only six weeks before, and of whom but a hundred and twenty had enough purpose of heart to follow on to Pentecost. And still He could say, "Yet surely My judgment is with the Lord, and My work with My God." And though Israel was "not gathered," He was "glorious in the eyes of the Lord" and "made His salvation to the ends of the earth." For it was life that had been sown.

So no matter, if we never see the full up-springing on earth of the Spirit-seed scattered. It is all the more likely that God may trust us with a great multiplying if our faith does not need to witness it. He can grant us spiritual harvests out of sight, of which He only gains the glory. In "the things which Christ hath ... wrought by us ... by the power of the Spirit of God" there is a multiplying energy that can reach, not single souls only, but other souls through them: a Holy Ghost touch that can fire trains, so to speak, far reaching beyond the sphere of what we see or know.

Such is the power of multiplication in the earthly seeds that it needs a constant battle, and the survival of the fittest, to keep us from being overrun with one and another. The henbane, for instance (by no means the most prolific) would, they say, if every seed had its way every year for five years, produce from a single plant ten thousand billions--enough to cover the whole area of the dry land of the world, allowing seventy-three plants to the square metre.[footnote*: "Natural History of Plants"--Kerner and Oliver] Perhaps God permits the seeming waste of such an overwhelming proportion of the seed formed, to show us the Fountain of Life that there is in Him; and to teach us that there is no straitening in the Spirit of the Lord. "There is no limit" (as someone has said) "to what God can do with a man, provided he will not touch the glory."

And God's possibilities for these germs of Spirit-life are not bound by time. Jesus is drawing so near that already our thoughts and hopes begin to step over the shrinking foreground of "the present age," and to rest in the ever-opening horizon beyond. Who can tell what harvest after harvest may be waiting in the eternal years, after the summer of earth has faded into the far past?

Yes, we have to do with One Who "inhabiteth" eternity and works in its infinite leisure. Some years ago, when a new railway cutting was made in East Norfolk, you could trace it through the next summer, winding like a blood-red river through the green fields. Poppy seeds that must have lain buried for generations had suddenly been upturned and had germinated by the thousand. The same thing happened a while back in the Canadian woods. A fir-forest was cut down, and the next spring the ground was covered with seedling oaks, though not an oak-tree was in sight. Unnumbered years before there must have been a struggle between the two trees, in which the firs gained the day, but the acorns had kept safe their latent spark of life underground, and it broke out at the first chance.

And if we refuse to stay our faith upon results that we can see and measure, and fasten it on God, He may be able to keep wonderful surprises wrapt away in what looks now only waste and loss. What an up-springing there will be when heavenly light and air come to the world at last, in the setting up of Christ's kingdom! The waste places may see "a nation born in a day."

All that matters is that our part should be done. We are responsible for sowing to the Spirit--responsible, with an awful responsibility, that power should be set free in our lives, power that shall prevail with God and with men--responsible like the seed-vessel, for fulfilling our ministry to the last and uttermost. Let the cry be on our hearts, as it was on the heart of Jesus, to "finish the work" that the Father has given us. "My meat is to do the will of Him that sent Me, and to finish His work." On He went with it, though it cost Him the strong crying and tears of Gethsemane to fight through to the end--to live on to the "It is finished" of Calvary.

Is it our souls' hunger and thirst that, before He comes, we may have given every message He had for us to deliver--prevailed in every intercession to which He summoned us--"distributed" for His kingdom and "the necessity of saints" every shilling He wanted--shared with Him every call to "the fellowship of His sufferings" for others--pouted out His love and sympathy and help as He poured them out on earth? Are we longing that He should find when He comes no unspent treasure, no talent laid up in a napkin, like the unshed seed in its shelly fold? Are we acting as if it were our longing? "By Him actions" (not longings) "are weighed!"

Take one more look at our meadow. The summer days are cooling down, and the storms have begun to come. The ground is bare and blackened, the stalks and leaves are battered to shreds: but seeds are everywhere. The earth is strewn with the husks. Whence they come none can tell, and they are broken down into nothingness. All is death--death reigning. The first showers are only bringing in a fresh stage of it where all seemed dead before, beating them, bleached and weather-worn and split, into the softened mould. Everything is quiet, for the seeds have gone down into the resting stage through which they all have to pass, whether it is during the frost in England, or the burning African summer. Do we not know the counterpart in the inner world, when Spirit-seed has been shed, and a strange waiting-time comes in which nothing happens--a silence on God's part in which death has to be allowed to reign before it is swallowed up in victory?

But all is on the very verge of a flood-tide of life, for the seed-vessel has reached its highest ministry now. The last wrappings are torn, and from every rent and breach the bare grain is shed forth and brought into direct contact with the soil: and suddenly, as if by miracle, the quickening comes, and the emerald shoot is to be seen.

Can we read our last lesson? Here, in service, we see the same goal being reached as in the soul's inner history. Both end in absolute simplicity, in Christ alone. For the highest aim of ministry is to bring His immediate presence into contact with others-- so to bring Him and them face to face that He can act on them directly, while we stand aside, like John the Baptist, rejoicing greatly.

We used to look at our inner life as separate from our service: but as we go on they merge into one--Christ--the same Christ; whether folded to our hearts in His secret temple, like the seed in its husk, or set free in contact with those around to carry on His quickening work--all and only Christ.

"Christ the beginning, and the end is Christ." We saw how the soul's first step is to let Him in as its life: the last step in a sense can go no further. It is only that the apprehension of Him has increased, and the hindrances and limitings have been swept away.

Christ--Christ--Christ--filling all the horizon. Everything in us: everything to us: everything through us. "To live is Christ."--Amen.

Made in the USA
Lexington, KY
07 November 2018